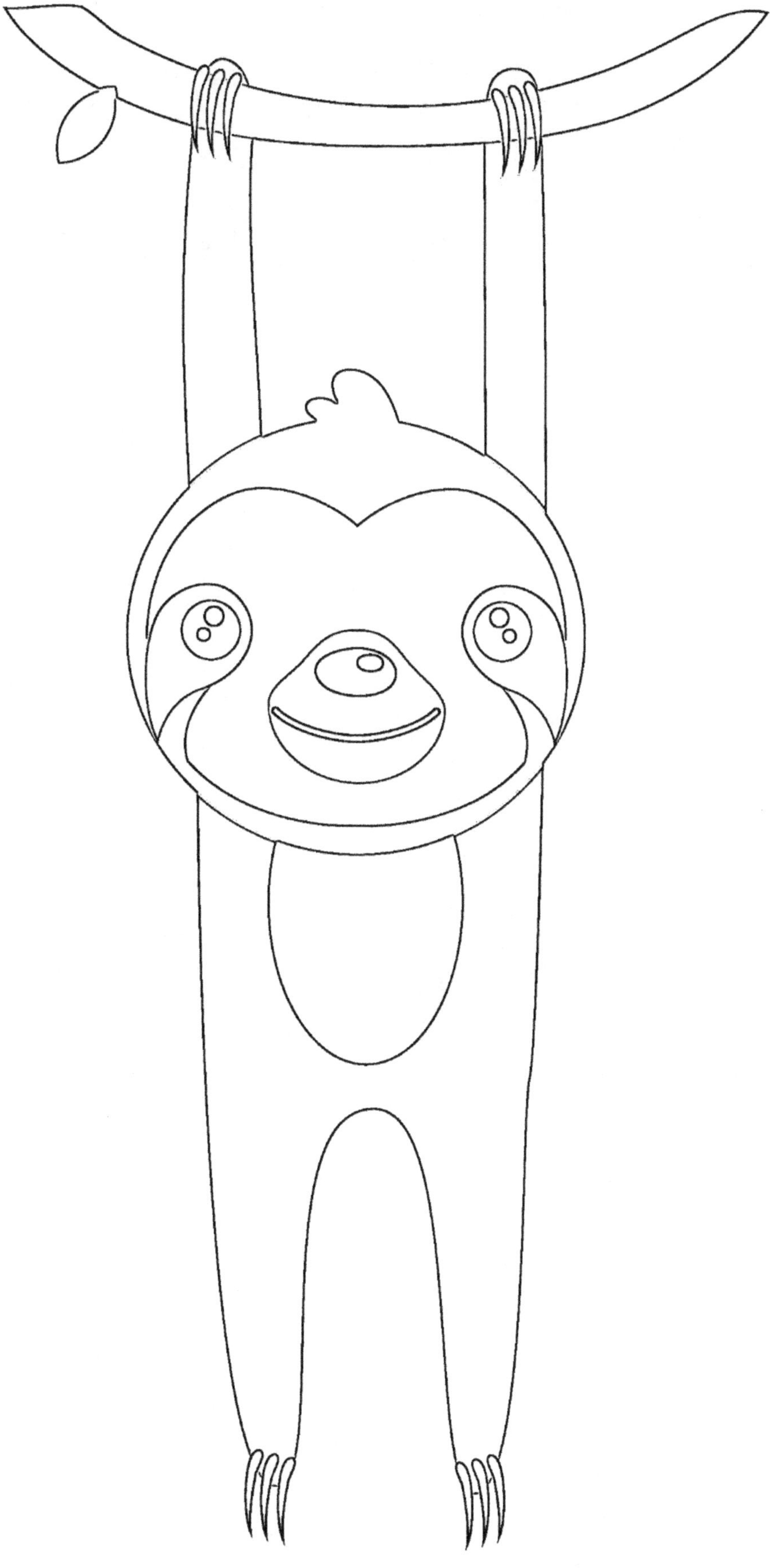

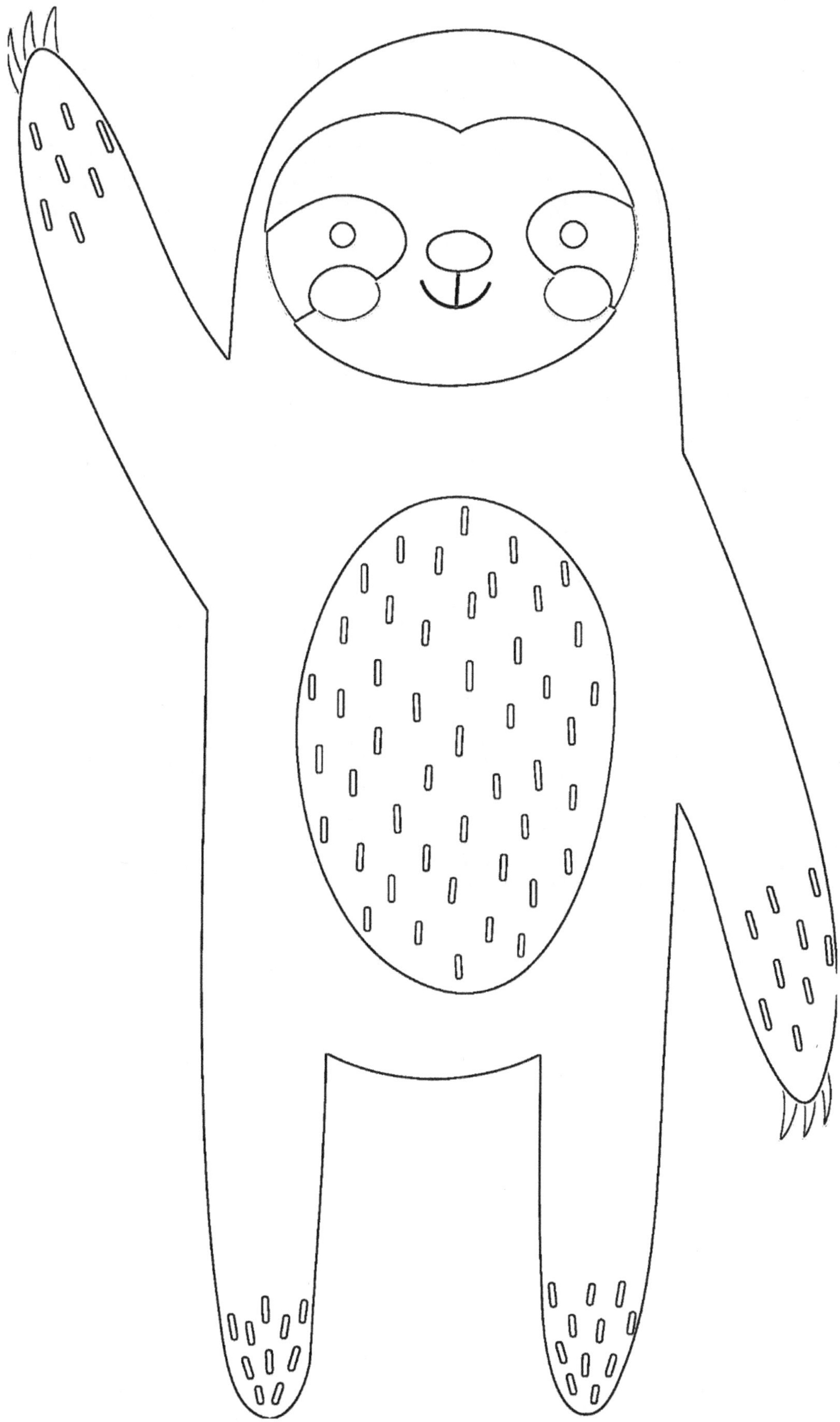

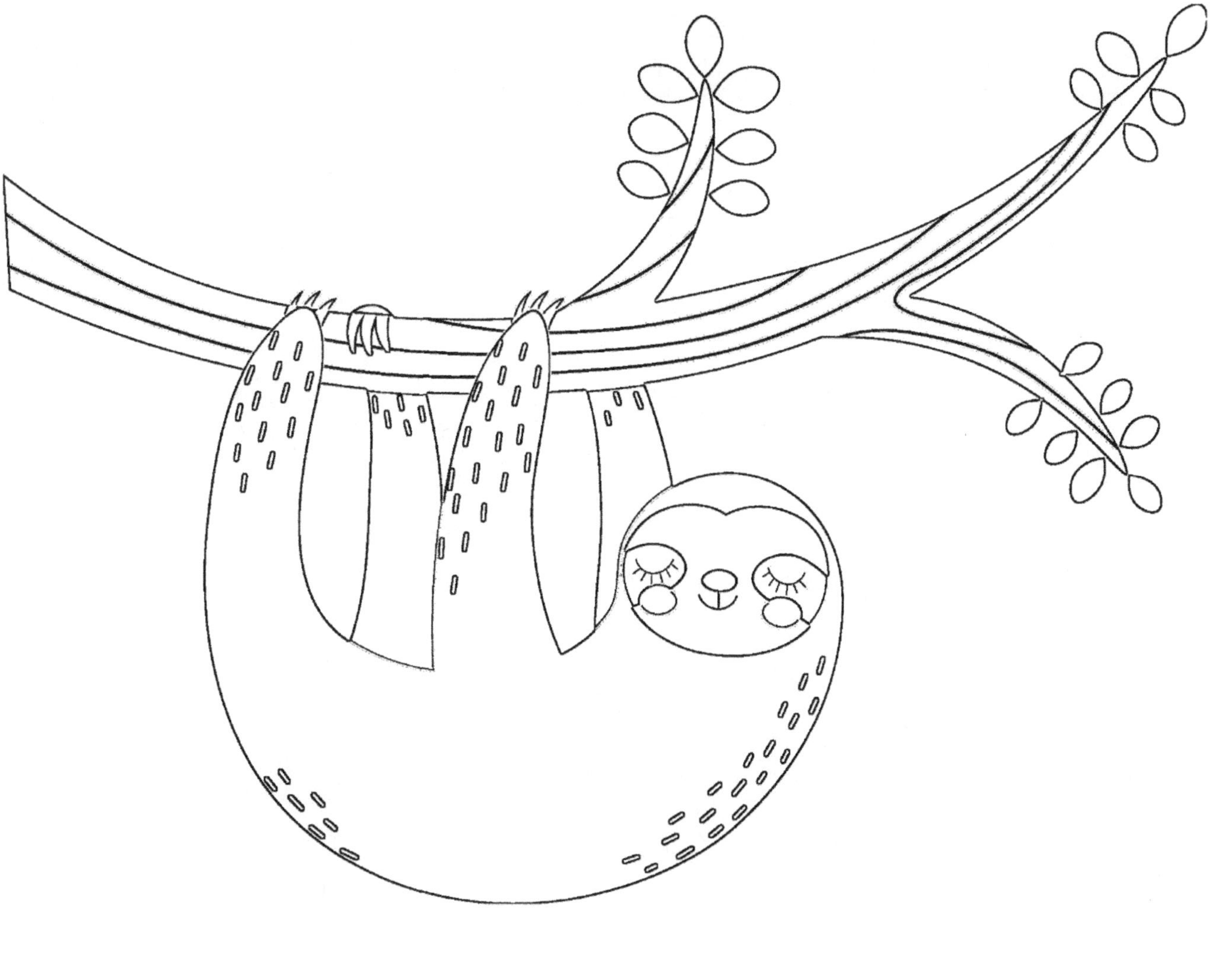

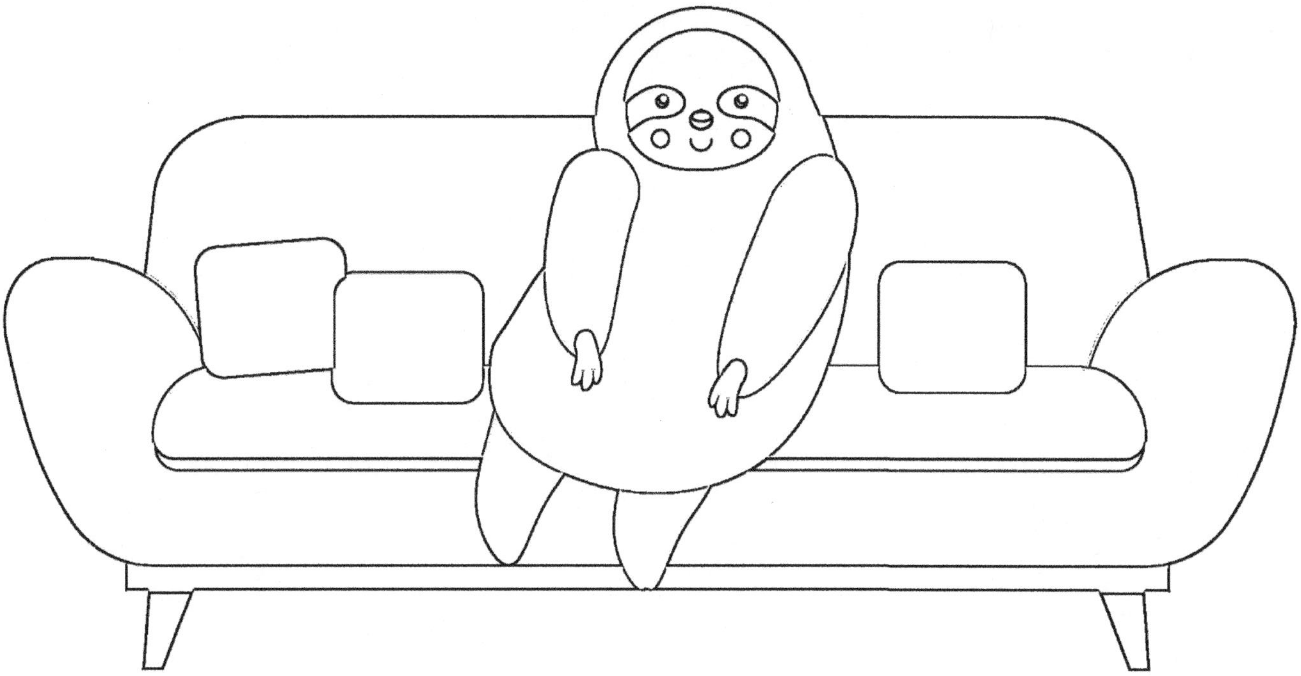

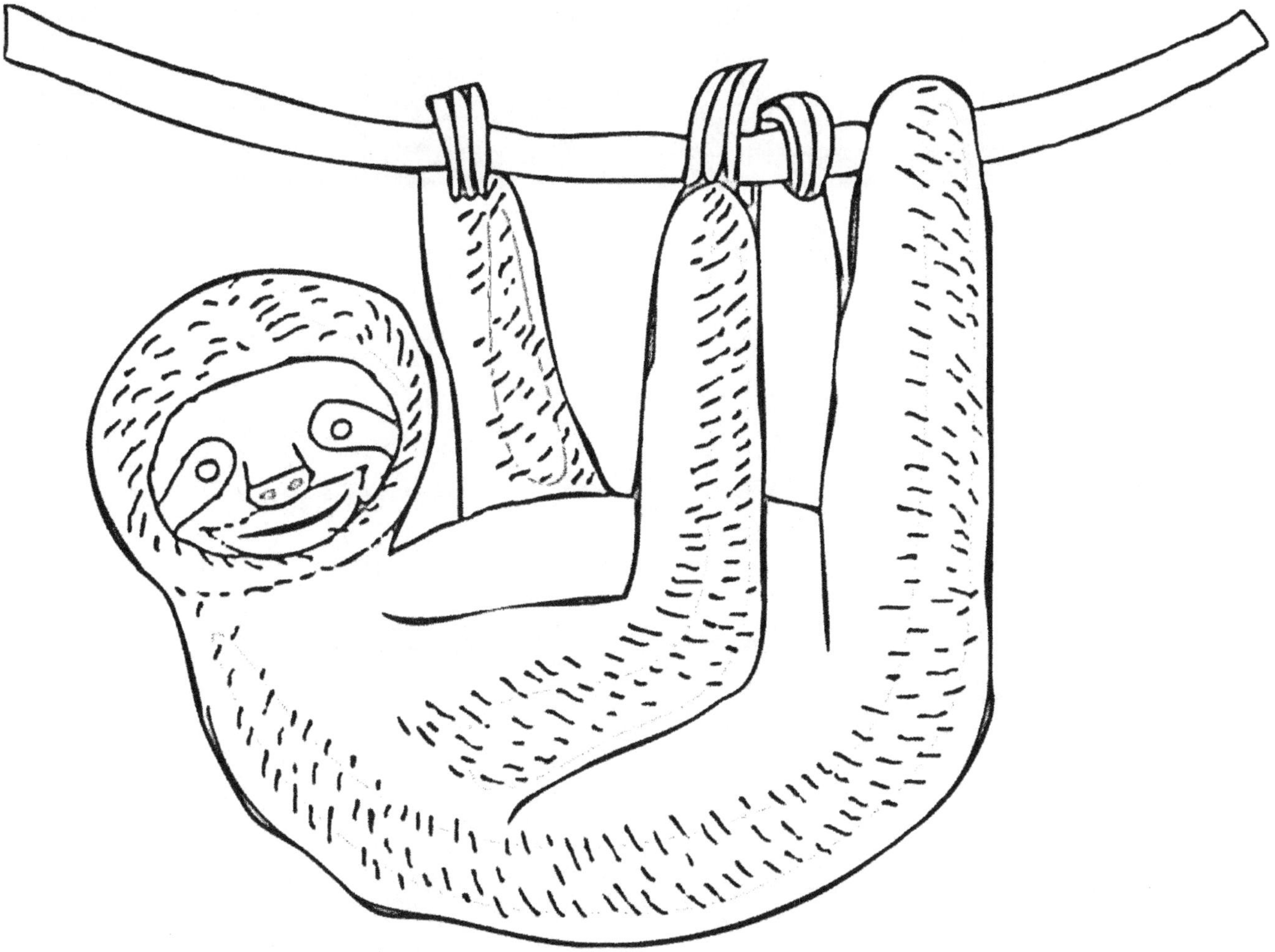

Made in the USA
Las Vegas, NV
19 July 2024

92628583R00031